Lantern Festival

T0362808

Time To Spend With Your Family

It is the Lantern Festival.
Lantern Festival is a time
to be with our family.

We will see lots of lanterns.

Some lanterns are big.

Some lanterns are little.

Look at this lantern.

It is like a dragon.

This lantern is like a lion.

Look at the dancers.

They are dancing on **stilts**.

The stilts make them very, very high.

9

Here are the men playing the drums. They will play the drums for the dancers.

Here are the men playing the **cymbals**. They will play the cymbals for the dancers.

Lantern Festival

is special for us.

Glossary

cymbals

stilts